THIS BOOK BEL

We get to serve

NAME: _____

DATE: _____

WE GET TO SERVE

Copyright (C) 2025 by We Get to Serve Books. All rights reserved.

No part of this book may be used or represented in any manner without the written permission of the author except for the use of brief quotes in a book review.

International Standard Book Number: 979-8-9988551-3-9

For more information and books , visit us online at www.wegettoservebooks.com

About The Author

Dr. Colleen Damon is a pioneer in creative faith-based wellness, combining the science of neuroplasticity with the healing power of service, reflection, and artistic expression. With over 25 years of experience in missions and trauma-informed care, she designs tools that promote emotional resilience, spiritual growth, and brain renewal. As the founder of We Get To Serve (WGTS) Books, Dr. Colleen merges her academic background—holding a doctorate in Missiology and Cultural Anthropology and a master's in Human Resource Management—with her passion for healing through creativity. Her therapeutic resources, including coloring books, gratitude journals, and reflection workshops, are grounded in the belief that the brain can rewire itself through intentional habits, prayer, and creative engagement. Whether used in counseling settings, recovery programs, or personal quiet time, her materials remind us that transformation is always possible—and that we don't have to serve, We Get To. Learn more at www.wegettoservebooks.com

Dedication

This book is lovingly dedicated to every woman who finds herself on the journey of recovery- from trauma, addiction, grief/loss, heartbreak, or anything that once tried to break her spirit.

To the one rebuilding her life, relearning how to trust herself and others…

To the one rediscovering her faith, her voice, her worth…
This is for you.
May each page bring you a moment of peace, a breath of courage, and a whisper from Heaven that you are not alone-you are deeply loved and divinely purposed.

We created this book with you in mind. Because healing is holy, and coloring is calming. Because your story matters. And because in this sacred journey…
We don't have to recover alone-We Get To, together!

We Get To Serve Books

1 Peter 5:10 (NIV)
And the God of all grace… will himself restore you and make you strong, firm and steadfast.

Finding HER: A Journey of Recovery & Purpose

There is a quiet beauty in every season of a woman's life — a sacred journey of becoming, of beholding, and of being found.
Finding Her in recovery is more than discovering a style, a voice, or a dream.
It is awakening to the truth that we are created with purpose, shaped by grace, and called to serve with the gifts God has placed within us.

At every stage — whether stepping into adulthood, navigating the changes of midlife, or embracing the richness of senior years — we are invited to lean in, listen, and love who we are becoming.

We don't have to have it all figured out. We don't have to walk alone.
We Get To Grow. We Get To Rise. We Get To Serve.

As you color each page, pause to reflect on how far you've come during your journey of recovery...

And remember: **You are still finding her** — and you are right on time.

Dr. Colleen N. Damon-Duval

HE DID IT JUST FOR ME

We Get To Serve Books

🌿 WGTS Prayer for Women in Recovery

"I Get To Heal, I Get To Hope"

Dear Lord,

Thank You for never giving up on me.

Even when I felt lost, You saw me.

Even when I was broken, You were mending me with mercy.

Thank You for this season of healing, this chance to begin again.

I lift every regret, every pain, every mistake to You,

And I receive Your forgiveness, grace, and love.

Help me walk in newness—not in shame, but in strength.

Let Your Word be the light that guides me.

Let my hands be used to serve, not to harm.

Let my heart be restored, not hardened.

Remind me daily that I am chosen, cherished, and changed by You.

I may not know every step ahead,

But I trust the One who walks with me.

In You, I rise. In You, I recover.

In You, I get to be me.

Amen.

Dr. Colleen N. Damon-Duval

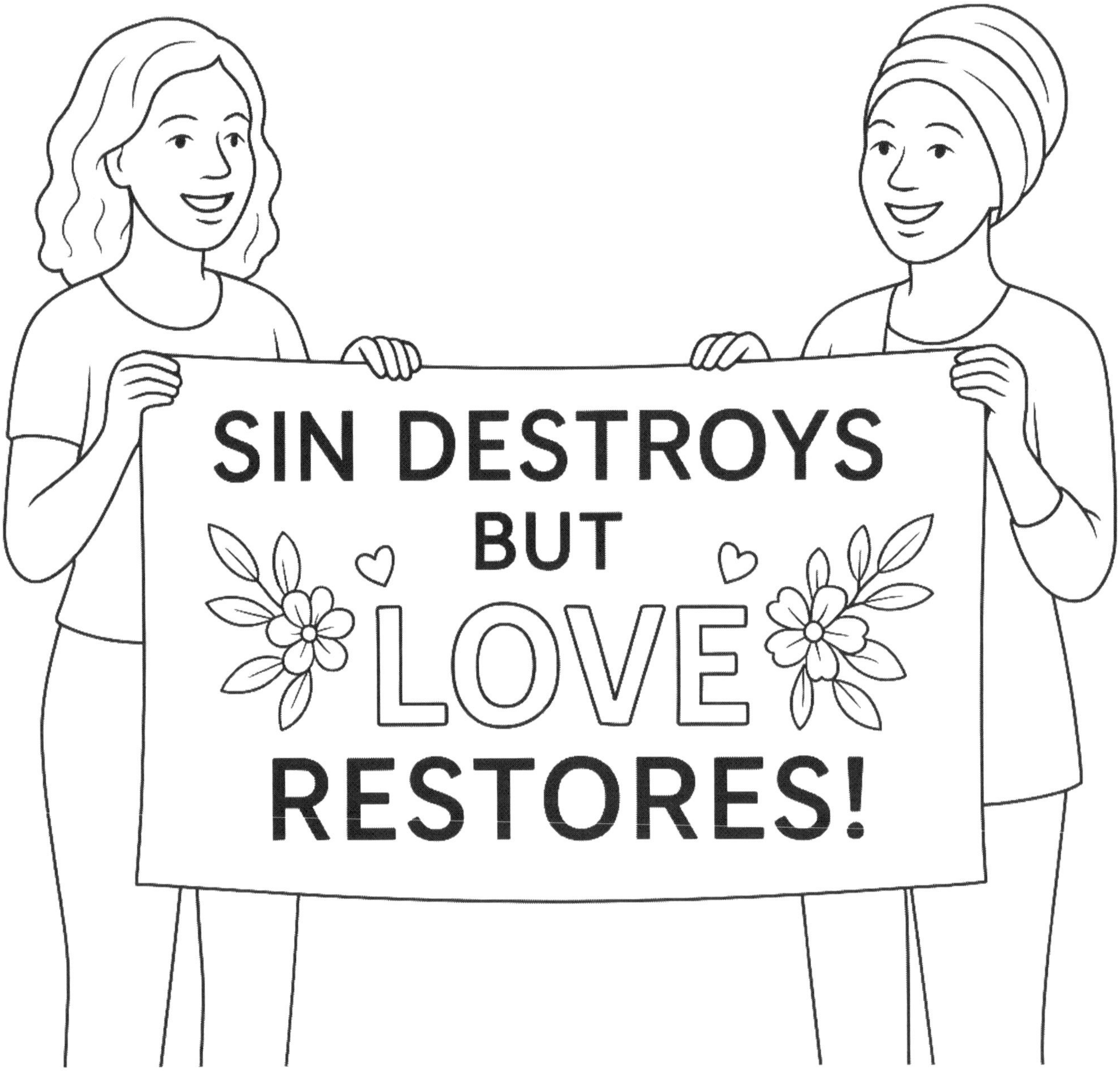
SIN DESTROYS
BUT
LOVE
RESTORES!

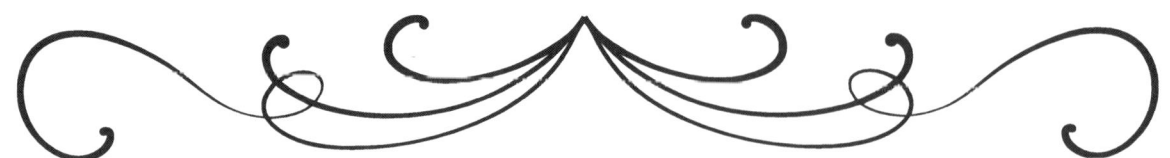

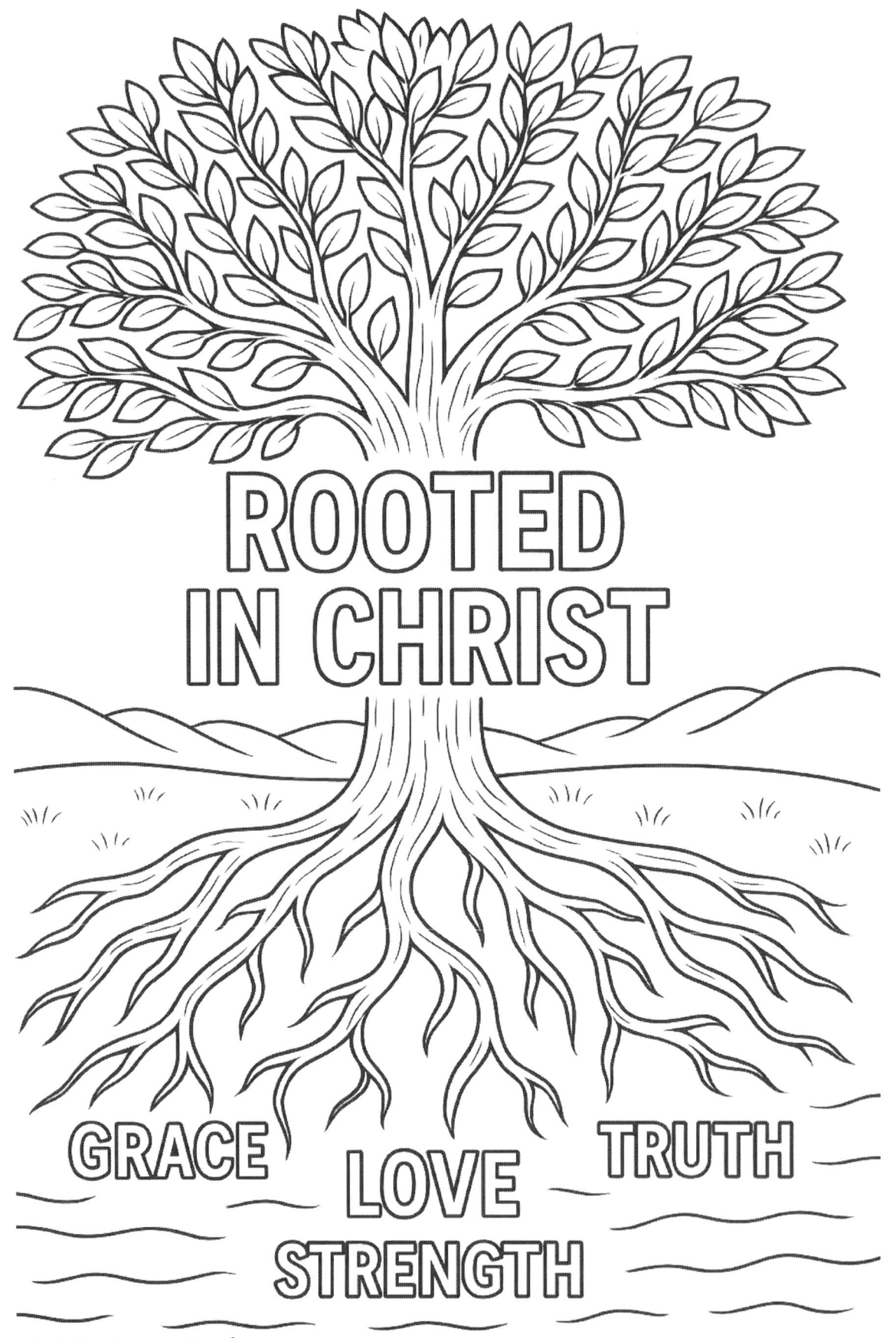

Held in His Arms

"The Lord is close to the brokenhearted
and saves those who are crushed in spirit."

Psalm 34:18

Peace Trusting in God

You Got This!

Hebrews 11:1 (NIV)

Now faith is confidence in what we hope for and assurance about what we do not see.

Jeremiah 30:17 (NIV)

"But I will restore you to health and heal your wounds," declares the Lord.

WGTS Poem: "She Rises Again"

She is not who the world said she was–
She is who God is calling her to become.
From the ashes of shame, she rises in grace,
With a new light of hope shining in her face.
She traded the weight of regret for release,
Now walking in healing, in wholeness, in peace.
Each step is a victory, each breath a new song,
She's learning that broken can still become strong.
She is not forgotten, not too far gone–
She is seen, she is held, she is being reborn.
With hands lifted high and a heart made new,
She declares: "God, I belong to You."
So when doubt tries to whisper, "You'll never be free,"
She answers with faith: "God is restoring me."
Because now she knows what it means to forgive,
To hope, to believe, and to truly live.
She's no longer surviving–
She's serving, she's healing, she's thriving.

Dr. Colleen N. Damon-Duval

1 Peter 5:10 (NIV)

And the God of all grace··· will himself restore you and make you strong, firm and steadfast.

Joel 2:25 (NIV)

"I will repay you for the years the locusts have eaten…"

Creative Therapy: Peace In The Process

Thou wilt keep her in perfect peace whose mind is stayed on thee. Isaiah 26:3

A Whispered Prayer

Lord, thank You for the woman I am becoming.

Help me to trust the journey, love the process,

and serve with a heart full of grace.

Finding HER is a gift

and today, I receive it with joy.

Amen.

Psalm 147:3 (NIV)
He heals the brokenhearted and binds up their wounds.

Blessed is she who has believed that the Lord would fulfill His promises to her.

Luke 1:45

We Get To Serve Books 39

PRAYER CHANGES THINGS!

Thank you for purchasing this coloring book. Checkout our website for other creative therapy content and check out our weekly blog to learn more about the impact of science and faith-based creative content.

We would love for you to leave us a comment. We are available for group and organization sessions, speaking engagements and team building activities. We can also personalize content to meet your needs. See You In The Next Book. HTTPS:wegettoservebooks.com

We Get To Serve Books

Made in the USA
Middletown, DE
31 October 2025

20401890R00024